One Bead at a Time
Exploring Creativity with Bead Embroidery

Robin Atkins

One Bead at a Time
Exploring Creativity with Bead Embroidery

Beadwork, photography and text by Robin Atkins

Copyright© January, 2000
Revised Edition: September, 2000; Additional Printings: 2000, 2002, 2004

ISBN: 0-9705538-2-X

This edition printed by: Bang Printing, PO Box 587
Brainerd, MN 56401; 1-800-328-0450.

Tiger Press
837 Miller Road
Friday Harbor, WA 98250
tigerpress@interisland.net

IN MEMORY OF MY FATHER:
CLIFFORD ATKINS
(1914 - 1947)

DEDICATED TO MY BROTHER:
THOMAS ATKINS
friend, sculptor, and kindred bead artist

ACKNOWLEDGEMENTS:

This book would not exist without the inspiration, trust,
and feedback provided by my students over the past 12 years.
Nor would I be where I am in my artistic development,
if it were not for the mentorship, love, and sharing
of my friend, Carol Berry.

I thank my partner, Robert Demar,
and my long-time friend, Elizabeth Chenoweth,
for their continuing patience and support
of all my artistic endeavors.

I thank my five "Creativity Sisters:" Mary Preston, Carol Berry,
Suzanne Kjelland, Marilyn Fogelquist, and Carol Peringer;
also - Anna Feher, Kathy Taylor, Lori Talcott, and Linn Jacobs -
for many years of shared encouragement.

I thank my family, Shelley Tucker (my poetry teacher),
Tim Hulley, all those who have hired me to teach, Rosanne and
Chuck Taylor, Candy Hoeschen, Terri Atwell, Terri Stueve . . .
and the list could fill all the pages of this book.

"Generations"
3" x 5" drawstring pouch

This was the first piece I made using the concept of
improvisational bead embroidery.

Bead Magic

In this book, you will see how beads, creativity, and healing are related. You will learn to stitch beads on fabric improvisationally, creating art work which is compelling, inspired, beautiful, fun, and satisfying to make. You will discover ways to break through the walls of doubt and criticism that prevent us from exploring our full artistic potential. This book is about improvisational bead embroidery as a pathway to greater creativity and source for personal healing. My intent is to inspire and to teach.

Let's begin with the magical quality of beads! If you want creativity, if you want to develop your artistic abilities, work with beads. They are inherently creative. Just think of the infinite variety:

> colors - every hue and shade you can imagine
> materials - glass, stones, pearls, wood, shell, metal, plastic,
> paper,fabric, rose petals (yes, really!), fossils,
> clay, seeds, bone, horn, felted wool, etc.
> opacity - from totally transparent to opaque
> texture & finish - rough, smooth, frosted, glossy, soft, hard
> size - from smaller than a pin head to larger than a fist
> shape - round, oval, cubical, tubular, etc.; irregular
> forms; faceted shapes; and many special shapes such
> as heart, melon, leaf, flower, drop, ring, disc, etc.

And, as if that isn't enough, imagine all the things you can use with beads, particularly when you're doing bead embroidery. For example, in the work pictured here, you may find: buttons, sequins, bells, postage stamps, paper money, charms, feathers, coins, cabochons, ribbons, lace - and this list could go on too. In fact, beads offer the

"East & West"
6½" x 7½", leather bag (with fabric dolls), front and back views

6

greatest variety of any artistic medium. You can be like a child in a castle, every room filled with unique, challenging and beautiful toys, and hours to play with them.

There's something else that's special about beads which makes them magical - their history and their origins. Where have they been? Where and by whom were they made? Who has handled and worn and loved them? How old are they? What will their future be? You see, beads are long lasting and nearly ubiquitous. They are one of mankind's earliest artifacts, along with pots for cooking, and primitive tools. Archeologists tell us that beads are found in nearly every culture and every land since the first people walked on earth 40,000 years ago through the present. The beads of our history are like a kaleidoscope, each small bead used and reused to create beautiful objects. Whether conscious or not, these considerations impart a magnetism and charm to beads, making them hard to resist, and helping to bring out the creative force in you and me.

So, what I'm saying is: when you work with beads, you already begin with a half-full deck, maybe more. The variety, history, and origins of the beads you choose inherently contribute to the overall appeal of your work.

In my 12 years of teaching beadwork, many students guiltily "admit" they have bought more beads than they'll ever use. Or, they tell me they can not buy more beads until they finish the projects they've started. Some think they have to sell their work in order to "justify" their "habit." Many say they are "addicted to beads." In answer to this kind of thinking, I believe the following:

- Beads are good therapy and much cheaper than a therapist.
- Beads bring beauty and a creative force to our lives that is healing and nurturing.

- You and I are worth it; and we don't have to sell our work
  to prove it!
- Beads are valuable, whether they're in a drawer, on your
  works-in-progress, or on a finished piece.
- Making things with beads, even simply holding or looking
  at them, connects us to our artistic side, our
  creative force.

The Creative Force

What do you believe about creativity? What's your first, instinctive reaction when I ask you, "Are you a creative person?" Most of us get a little frightened by that question. An inner voice says, "Yes, of course I am a creative person." But our ever-present critical and fearful side often dominates with a resounding, "No, not me..."

We are, by nature, creative. Our minds are capable of both convergent thinking, which makes order of things (and feels very proper or safe) and divergent thinking, which gives us novelty and inspiration (but feels scary). As children at play, we move freely between both ways of thinking. But, as we get into school, the emphasis turns more to making order, lining up the facts in a sensible or predictable way. In this stage of our lives, divergent thinking may be unrewarded or even punished. We learn to stay in line and hold hands, and that 2 + 2 always equals 4. Yet couldn't we just as easily learn and practice improvisation, invention or intuition along with the rules and formulas? So, in our school years, for many of us, the creative side begins to shut down, more in some than in others. We must realize, however, that it's still there, still a huge capacity within us, which we can release, develop and nurture. With a little effort, we can learn to be more creative at any age.

"Gusset Pouch"
4" x 5", front and back views

This little pouch is lined with ultrasuede light, which I also used to make side gussets (so the pouch opens wider). Although the bead embroidery is totally improvisational, I did not work with a theme or issue in mind. My only goals were to use beads and fabric I love, and to not get bored (have fun) working on it. The pouch shape comes from an old (early 1900) leather money pouch.

Breaking Walls

"I am an artist." I never thought I'd say or write, or even think these words. I grew up believing that my brother was "THE artist" in the family, and that a family could produce only one artist. I made pretty things too, but only because it's "what all girls do". And, of course, "all artists are born with their talent in full bloom". These beliefs formed a solid wall of opposition against any wish I ever had to take a drawing or painting class, or to write poetry and sing solos. They made me tell people, "Oh, I may be a good craftsperson, but never an artist. I don't have any original ideas. I'm not very creative." Sound familiar?

Doing beadwork these past years - churning out piece after piece, not to sell, but to please myself, being stimulated by customers, students and artist friends, working from my heart - put a crack in those beliefs and opened me to a glorious new world. I'm writing about this for those of you who, like I was, are stuck facing a wall of "can't do" about your artistry.

Here's what I believe is the real truth about artists and creativity. Each of us is an artist inside. Artistry is learned - mostly by practice, by doing it one piece at a time, not judging what we do, and moving quickly onto the next piece.

We get in touch with our artistry when we let go of our fear of failure and let our hearts speak out boldly, saying "This is what I like; I do it because I like it!" Journaling helps too. "The Artist's Way, A Spiritual Path to Higher Creativity," by Julia Cameron, taught me to journal and helped me in more ways than I can say. Also, doing our art with a small group of like-minded friends is important, because we support each other as artists.

And finally, we must appreciate just how valuable our creativity is to ourselves, our families, and ultimately the world. We don't short-change it; we take time to nurture it regularly. We go to museums, take workshops, buy books, pay for supplies - whatever it takes to keep practicing our art and breaking down the walls.

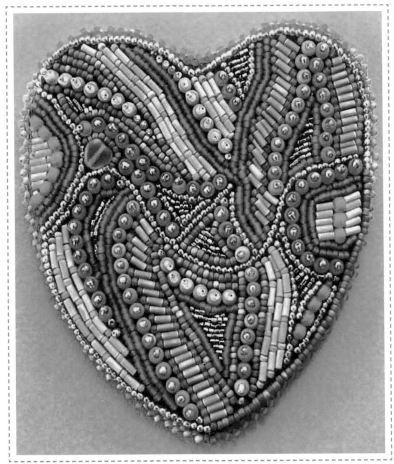

R. Atkins, 1994

"First Love"
4" x 4 ½", heart shaped bag

Working Improvisationally

Over the years, I've found that one of the best ways to break down the walls, the barriers to creativity, is to work improvisationally. When we follow the designs, patterns, and ideas of others, no matter how well we do it, our work doesn't look or feel very inspired. When we try to develop our own designs, we get better results and feel better about our work. But, many times in the process of planing, we run into walls or get blocked with judgements. Sometimes we try too hard. We over-work our designs, trying to make them fit all the "rules" we've learned for "successful art". I say "we", because it happens to most artists I know, including me. Most of us have had the experience of planning a project, carefully shopping for materials which "match" perfectly, spending hours trying various combinations, only to view our finished work as uninspired. An effective way to reduce this problem is to work improvisationally.

Although we can approach any type of art improvisationally (dance, drama, music, poetry, painting, etc.), my exploration of the concept centers on beadwork, especially bead embroidery. In the following pages, I will share with you some of the things I've discovered about improvisational bead embroidery, photographs of my work, and some of the unexpected personal benefits from working in this way. St. Francis of Assisi said something like: "He who works with his hands is a laborer; he who works with his hands and his mind is a craftsman; he who works with his hands and his mind and his heart is an artist." And that last is the biggest advantage of working improvisationally: it gets us back in touch with our hearts; it reveals our hearts' messages. In the process, we produce something "real," something that has more than beauty, more than interest; something that has heart and, therefore, life itself!

"Visual Jazz Fusion"
by
Carol Berry

This 3" x 3" square of improvisational bead embroidery, by Carol
Berry, is one square in a wall-
quilt, shown complete on page
16. Eight of us "bad, bad beaders" got together one day. Each
of us made and titled one square.
Later I put them together in a
wall piece, entitled "Ladies of the
Bad, Bad Bead."

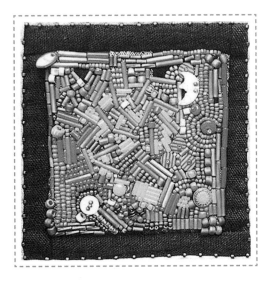

Improvisational Bead Embroidery

Improvisational
doesn't necessarily mean abstract.

It just means working without a plan,
with no design and no outcome, either on paper or in your mind.

The concept of improvisational bead embroidery was introduced to
me in the early '90s by Carol Berry, who is a jeweler and bead/fiber
artist. The idea is to work without a pattern or design, sometimes
without any plan for the outcome at all. Select fabric for the project
because you like it, without regard to "proper" fiber content or colors. Get in touch with the child within you. Take her (or him) to
the fabric shop and let her buy a quarter yard of anything which
pleases her. As you work, ask your inner child which bead she'd like
to sew next. Don't get in her way and don't be critical of her choices
or of how straight she sews. Just let her play. Like children's art

(only with all of your added years of experience and training in what makes things beautiful, artful, and intriguing), the results will have great spontaneous character.

My best work, I believe, is done this way. I select some fabric and some beads I love, choose a bead that appeals to me (without concerning myself about why it is calling me) and sew it on somewhere. Then I pick another bead, and another, until something tells me I'm finished.

I never let myself get bored. If I begin to get tired of a certain stitch or bead type or bead color, I try to recognize my sense of boredom right away and switch to something that feels more compelling. It's hard. My tendency is to want to hold onto a safe, predictable pattern. But if it's boring to do, isn't it possible that it will be just as boring to view?

"Ecstasy"

I made this 3" x 3" square for a group project, the "Ladies of the Bad, Bad Bead" wall-hanging quilt. I chose the theme of "ecstasy" before I started the piece, thinking that working with beads is, after all, pure ecstasy. I began with the large spiral button, and worked outward. When I look at it now, the energy of the ecstasy seems to be breaking through the "walls" of the border, just like my beliefs about creativity and artistry.

R. Atkins, 1993

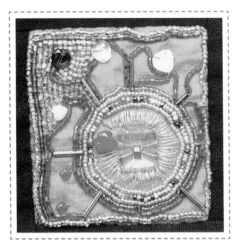

clockwise, from top left:

"il risveglia" (the rebirth) by Maria Porteous, *"Joy"* by Wilma Bishop,
"Bead Journey" by Brionie Williams, *"Bead Blooms"* by Suzanne Kjelland

These four squares, each 3" x 3", were made by four of my students to be included
in the wall piece, "Ladies of the Bad, Bad Bead," a group project shown on page 16.
We had so much fun beading that day - eight of us - stitching,
talking, and laughing together. All of us worked improvisationally, without a
plan, other than to make a 3 inch square. Some of us chose a theme concept
before beginning; others let the finished work inspire the name.

"Ladies of the Bad, Bad Bead"
16" x 25", wall hanging
with individual squares made by eight different women

16

Sometimes I decide to let my subconscious mind play with a theme or current issue in my life while I work. Some examples of themes in my work include: my Dad's death when I was 5 years old, menopause, money issues, relationships with various family members and friends, and marriage. I don't do anything more than recognize that the work may somehow be related to a certain theme. Bead embroidery is meditative, calming, and healing for me, especially when I let it be a "happening" rather than try to control it. In the following pages, you will see some examples of my work which have come out of an initial theme, and I'll explain how you can do it too.

The results of working improvisationally may astonish you. It's my experience that everyone who tries it is absolutely delighted with the results of this concept. Many gain confidence in their artistic abilities, a new sense of empowerment with color and design, and a bridge from craft to art. It's not the only way to develop your creativity, but it works for a lot of people. I invite you to try it and see for yourself.

Over the years, I've taught many workshops and introduced many new and practiced beaders to the concept of working improvisationally. Most do amazing work on their very first piece. Once, the members in a small class liked each other so well, they decided they wanted a reunion. They, a couple of my friends, and I spent one day beading together in my studio, each of us making a 3" square of bead embroidery on a fabric of our choice. Later I made the squares into the wall quilt you see on the left. Except for Carol Berry and me, all were new to beading, the square being only their first or second piece. Yet, notice how all the squares are compelling and fun to examine. The quilt was exhibited at the Bellevue Art Museum (Washington state) in the "Ubiquitous Bead" show, where it received much attention.

Nitty-gritty of Choosing Your Fabric

To begin a bead embroidery project, I first select a fabric. Mostly I work on 100% cotton or silk. Generally I use previously unused fabrics, but sometimes it's neat to use material from an old garment. For example, I've had students who have worked on: a piece of fabric from their own baby blanket, their husband's old work pants, their wedding dress, their grandmother's bathrobe, their child's first birthday dress. Using fabric from something which has special meaning for you will increase the energy of your work, and perhaps its healing power (more on this subject later). I have also worked on leather (see "East & West" on page 6 and medicine bags on page 47), but it is difficult to get the detail I like, even on the finest leather. Some enjoy working on ultrasuede, but again, I prefer the softer hand and printed patterns available on cotton fabrics.

Speaking of printed patterns, most students at first prefer the idea of working on a plain colored fabric. But, I have found that using a print which really appeals to me, helps to bring more color and life into my work. The scale of the print influences the scale of my work; the mood of the print (playful, romantic, exciting, peaceful, etc.) influences the mood of my work; the colors influence my color choices, sometimes in directions I wouldn't normally go; and the design may also influence my work subconsciously. An example of this is shown on page 19.

Whatever fabric you consider, if there is anything (any little detail) you don't like about it, don't use it. Find one that appeals to you in every way. It should feel good, look good, and make you feel happy and excited about working with it. When in doubt, go with your first impression or your "gut level feeling."

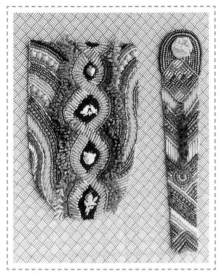 

"Marriage Bag"
front, back and sides; in progress

I have photographed the front, back and sides of this bag on the same fabric I used
to do the beadwork. When you study the two sets and look for the influence of
the fabric on my work, you can see that the pieces on the left are much more
geometric; while the ones on the right are more flowing and soft.

Nitty-gritty of Getting Started

After choosing fabric, I select a palette of beads, buttons, and other
embellishments, any of which I may or may not actually use. These I
put in a "project box", along with needles, thread, scissors, and a
small beading cloth.

I choose my beads quickly, without looking at my previously selected fabric, because I want my artistic side to make the choices.

I find that if I ponder too long, my intellectual side takes over, and I start wanting to match the fabric colors, or find beads that "go together." We are so influenced about color schemes by our culture, advertising, and clothing trends, that it's very difficult to be creative. Children, who are much less influenced by popular trends, will make choices simply according to what delights them. Try to let the "child in you" have a say in your selection.

To sew beads on fabric, you will need a means to keep the fabric from puckering as you work. While some use an embroidery hoop for this, I don't recommend it, because when the fabric relaxes after being stretched in the hoop, it may pucker and make your work look "lumpy." I use a paper backing, which I baste to the fabric. Generally I use acid-free interleaving paper (an archival paper available from many art supply stores), but any notebook or typing paper will do. Once, when making a piece about my "money issues," I used a $5 bill. As you work, the paper will become soft, until it's almost unnoticeable. When I finish my beading, I moisten, then tear away the excess paper from around the edge on the back. If you are doing bead embroidery on a garment, consider the "weight" of the fabric. For heavier fabric, such as denim, paper may not be needed. If you decide to use paper to back beadwork on a garment, washing (after the beadwork is completed) will soften and/or remove most of the paper backing.

If you know the finished size of your project, cut the fabric and paper big enough to allow a 1" margin on all sides. If the fabric frays easily (such as silk), turn under the raw edges of the fabric and baste, or zigzag on your sewing machine. You may not need all of the margin to finish your piece, but often it's handy. If you don't know what you want to make with your beadwork, or how big it will be, cut the fabric and paper to a reasonable working size (not much more than 12″ square, or it will be too cumbersome to hold.) Sometimes I have no idea what I'm going to make with my beadwork. At other times I have a specific shape in mind. (For example, the pattern for the bag shown on page 9 was taken from an old leather coin purse.) In this case, I draw the exact shape that I want the finished piece to be on the backing paper, then stitch along the pencil line with small basting stitches in a thread color which can be seen easily on the fabric side. I only sew beads inside the guidelines marked by my basting stitches.

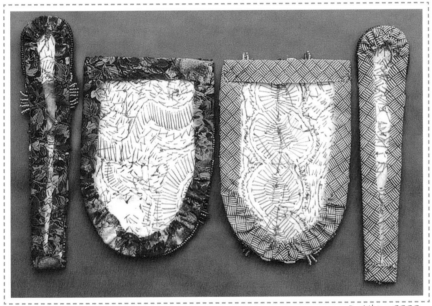

R. Atkins, 2000

"Marriage Bag"
work in progress, showing reverse side of pieces

This photo shows what the front, back and side pieces of a bag look like when the bead embroidery is complete. I tear off the extra paper around the edges of my beadwork, and turn under the fabric, ready to attach the lining. (See the right sides on pages 19, and 42-43.)

R. Atkins, 1994

"Songs of the Universe"
14" x 18" draw-string bag (detail below)

I had no idea where I was going with this
when I started. I first sewed on the
mother-of-pearl button, then the leaves
around it, then the diagonal red "s"shape.
Gradually as I worked, the button seemed
to be a sun. And as moons and stars fol-
lowed, the piece got its name. The finished square sat around for a while, until
finally one day I made a "log cabin" border, then quilted and completed the bag.

R. Atkins, 1994

"Just Do It"

When your fabric is ready, pick up a bead or button or anything you really love, and sew it on. Don't think about what or where. Just do it. This will sound over-simplified, but simply continue sewing on beads and other things you really love until your piece is finished.

I have to interject a story here about the best advice anyone ever gave me. I had been taking a poetry class for which there was to be a "public reading." I wanted to honor the poems I had written (and perhaps throw some "smoke" over the jitters I was feeling at the thought of reading my poems out loud in front of a group of strangers) by making an "artist's book." I had never made a book before and had no idea how to do it. I called an artist friend, Linn Jacobs, who creates absolutely delicious one-of-a-kind books, and asked her if she would tell or show me how I could make a book for my poems. Her answer? "Just do it. Just take some paper and scissors and glue, and do it." I kept asking for specifics, but couldn't get any other answer from her. That was her most precious gift to me, and hopefully I can pass it on to you. I took her words to heart, not only for making my first book, but for everything since then that I wanted to do, but wasn't sure how to do, or even had doubts that I could do.

So, that's exactly how to do improvisational bead embroidery. Pick up beads you love, and sew them somewhere on your fabric. You don't have to know how; just do it; any way that works is fine. If you need them, there are some basic techniques for sewing beads on fabric at the end of this book. But, don't be surprised if, by working improvisationally with a "just do it" mantra, you discover some new techniques, or at least variations on those shown, as you work.

Exploring Issues, Themes, and Relationships In Your Bead Work

One of the great things about improvisational beading is that you can let your subconscious "work" on something which is important to you without being obvious, and without even knowing much about it. All you need do is to decide that you are making a particular piece about some issue, theme, or relationship which is compelling for some reason (either understood or not understood) in your life right now. That's all you have to do. Just tuck that assumption in the back of your mind, and proceed to sew beads you love onto your fabric. I do this quite often, and find that it is very therapeutic and healing. I will share a few intimate stories about some of my beadwork in the following pages, but you should know it's perfectly OK (and still just as healing) to keep your personal process about your work completely to yourself.

I tumbled into the "exploring issues with beadwork" concept rather accidentally. In a workshop about creativity, the instructor, Suzanne Kjelland, asked us what we would save if there was a fire and we had one last trip into our burning house after all the humans and pets were out. The question disturbed me greatly. I kept thinking about many wonderful little things important people in my life had made and given to me. It troubled me that I didn't even know where some of these things were. So, I spent most of the next day finding all my "treasures," and decided I would make a bag for them, of course, with improvisational bead embroidery.

The result, as yet unfinished, is what you see to the right and on the next four pages. I began with the "in case of fire, save treasures from friends" theme in the back of my mind. After selecting a fabric with flowers on it, and starting to sew with beads I love, it was apparent I

"In Case of Fire"
5" x 6", in progress

I will appliqué this piece on a large bag, as yet unmade, to hold many smaller bags
containing "treasures" made for me by friends and family members.

was making a heart shape. When that happens, let it be. Improvisational means without pre-planning, not abstract. So a heart it was to
become, as you can see above. Well, I had so much fun thinking
about all the wonderful treasures, and the people who made them,

and so much fun working on the "In Case of Fire" bag, that soon I was thinking I would make a bag for each piece. And so began a very long-term project, which is still in progress. Although the large bag is not finished (because I don't know yet how big it will need to be to hold all of the smaller bags), all of the "treasures" are now safely in one place, where I can easily get them in case of fire.

After completing the central bead embroidery for the outer bag, I began to work on individual bags for each treasure. I thought to make the beadwork for each bag an abstract/improvisational picture of the person who gave me the treasure. I began with a booklet made for me by my friend and mentor, Carol Berry. Choosing a fabric that somehow (color, design, scale?) made me think of Carol, I began by sewing on a faceted black glass button. After sewing a circle of beads around it, I put an arc of dark blue beads under it.

Suddenly it looked like an eye; and I remembered something Carol often says about "three ways of seeing - that we see with our eyes, our hands, and our hearts." When I am working improvisationally, and something like that happens, I let it be. OK, so I made a heart around the eye and a hand around the heart, drawing an outline on the backing paper, and basting around the pencil lines so that I could see the stitches on the right side. Is this still improvisational? Mostly it is, because the colors chosen, and the background and fill for the shapes were unplanned. Since the completed square of bead embroidery was far too small to make into a bag big enough for the booklet, I added fabric strips to increase the size.

"Ways of Seeing"
7" x 7½", small flap and button closure

The bead embroidery on this bag is only 3 ¾" x 4". Fabric strips added, in "log cabin" quilting technique, extend the work to the intended size. I worked the bead embroidery on the same fabric as the outside border of the bag.

27

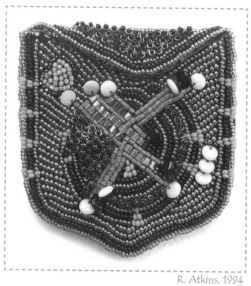

"Liz's Bag"
3″ x 3″, beaded both sides
flap snaps shut

R. Atkins, 1994

R. Atkins, 1997

"Emese's Pouch"
4 ½″ x 4 ½″, beaded both sides, opens like a coin purse

28

"*Chino's Bag*"
7 ½" x 9 ½"
flap and button closure

The size of the bead embroidery is only about 2 ½" square. Strips of fabric added to the square ("log cabin" technique from quilting), embellished with beads, make the bag its intended size.

Robin Atkins, 1993

R. Atkins, 1994

"*Mom's Pouch*"
5 ¾" x 5 ½", pouch is quilted with beads

R. Atkins, 1993   R. Atkins, 1993

"Margaret's Bag" (left) and "Layne's Bag" (right)
I made these bags for my nieces, when they were about 8 years old, so they'd
have a special place to put their secret treasures.

The bags shown on pages 28 and 29 (part of the "In Case of Fire" se-
ries) and the two above are all examples of improvisational bead embroidery which is intended vaguely to be about a specific person,
perhaps like an abstract "painting" of them. There is another possibility. Rather than focus your subconscious mind on a particular
person, you can focus on your relationship with this person. Although the former may contain elements of your relationship, the
shift in focus will alter your work considerably, and could open some
doors of insight for you. The best example of this is one of my

students, who began making a piece, thinking it would be about her mother, and that she would gift it to her mother when complete. After several days, she showed me her work. Using dark browns and black colors, she had sewn on beads on top of beads on top of beads until she had several mounds almost an inch high. "They look like cancer," she said in obvious distress, "like tumors..." When I asked her what she thought it was about, she replied that it seemed to be about her difficult relationship with her mother. I suggested she keep beading on the piece and see where it would lead her. Two weeks later she returned to show me her work. It was transformed; and so in some ways was she. She had removed every bead from her fabric (saying that this symbolized taking her bitter past from around her neck), and started again on the same fabric with pearly white beads, which soon began to look like a bird. So she let it become a "phoenix rising," which, she said, seemed to represent herself and "my new freedom from my oppressive past under my dominant mother's thumb."

Healing Old Wounds

In the story above, my student experienced tremendous healing of old wounds by working improvisationally with her beads, something I've seen again and again with my students and in my own work. It seems that when we bypass our orderly, controlling, critical mind, and allow our subconscious to work on an issue in our life (while simply playing with our beads), amazing things may happen. This is a little more difficult than it sounds, because as we work and our minds notice what's happening, we can easily become frightened and return to an intellectual approach to our work. I'll share with you two healing miracles in my life from working this way, and give you some hints about how to keep yourself on the healing track when the going gets rough and "the critical voice" begins to bark at you.

"Pathway to Daddy: Work of My Hands"
8" x 7 ½" bead embroidery, matted and shadow-box framed

Five days before my fifth birthday, my daddy was killed in an auto-
mobile accident. For good reasons, my mother decided the best
course of action was to let my paternal grandparents care for my
brother and me, while she returned to college. Since the school year
had just begun, we were packed up ready to move to another part of
the state immediately after the funeral, which we did not attend.
Two years later, mom married a wonderful man, who soon became

R. Atkins, 1995

"Remembering Daddy: The Key is Me"
8″ x 7 ½″ bead embroidery, matted and shadow-box framed

as dear to us as any father could be. Life went on; we are a happy,
loving family, unusually blessed with lasting good feelings between
us. About the time I was starting to work improvisationally with
beads, an old friend of my biological father - out of the blue - sent
me some photographs of him. Somehow, I recognized that my un-
expressed grief about his passing was, and always had been, a barrier
in my life. I decided to do an improvisational piece about my daddy.

First, I took one of the photos I had received and using a Xerox-transfer method, copied it on some fine silk fabric. Something compelled me to choose only white, off-white and silver beads for this project, though I told myself I could add color any time I wanted. Rummaging though my odds and ends of things, I also selected some buttons from my paternal grandfather's collection, an arctic tern's feather somebody had given me, a silver rabbit button, a silver key, and a small porcelain kitty button. I noticed that whenever I worked on the piece, I would feel calm, that the work itself was meditative and peaceful, that I was enjoying sewing white beads on white fabric with white thread. Without planning to do so, eventually I sewed all the things I had gathered on the piece. The little key had no holes through which to sew it on the fabric, so I used a piece of fine netting over it, beading over the netting around the key to hold it on the fabric. I remember feeling very satisfied about the way it looked, almost hidden at the bottom of the "picture" (see bottom center of "Remembering Daddy: The Key is Me," page 33). The feather is attached the same way.

When I finished, in about 3 ½ months, a door had opened within me. I found myself freely and easily writing poems about my childhood, especially about my daddy; memories surfaced and I wrote as a child in my journal about my experiences and grief at the time of his death. I felt a great sense of release, yet at the same time, a compulsion to keep sewing white beads on silk fabric. So I gathered more compelling things - more buttons, the nib of an old ink pen, the wishbone from a Cornish game hen - and began a second piece about daddy. By the time it was finished, I guess I must have finally soothed the grieving little girl in me, because it feels like the barrier is gone now, and I'm moving forward in certain areas of my life which were previously blocked. And, besides that, I haven't felt the need to "play" with little white beads for a long time. For a couple of years these two pieces remained in my "project box," until finally I framed them and hung them in my studio, where they are today.

Later, I began a second healing journey through a combination of journaling and improvisational bead embroidery. This time, the writing came first. Writing "stream of consciousness" (or you could call it improvisationally) in my journal, I surprised myself with a long list of "commandments" about money - things like: thou shall never borrow money; thou shall never have enough money; thou shall never trust people about money - and the list went on for several pages. I already knew I had money issues; in the past I'd even gone to a counseling seminar about money fears. But, here they were, big time, in my face. The next day, as I was teaching a bead embroidery class, I took a bill (happened to be $5) out of my purse and used it to back my new project - a piece about money issues. I found a piece of striped silk that reminded me of wealth, basted it on the $5 bill, selected some beads I liked, and started beading. At the time, I had no idea what I might do with the finished bill-shaped

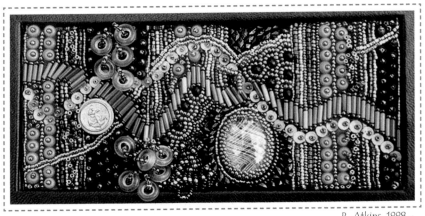

R. Atkins, 1998 -

"Money Madness" - 6" x 3", detail

R. Atkins, 1998 –

R. Atkins, 1998 –

R. Atkins, 1998 –

"Money Madness"
*9 ¹/₄" x 8" hand-bound artist's book, leather cover with inlaid bead embroidery,
real money fly-leaf and embellishments, rubber-stamped text, and collage*

36

piece of bead embroidery, only that as I worked on it, I would try to let my subconscious go wherever it wished. After beading the bill, my work sat around for over a year before one day I felt inspired to inlay the piece in the cover of a book When I finished binding the book, I began to write the commandments from my journal onto the pages by rubber-stamping the letters and embellishing the pages with money, papers, threads, etc. All this was powerful healing for me in many ways. Among other changes, I've been comfortable with not working (for the first time in my teen through adult life) while I learned how to use my computer (purchased with my savings, I might add) so I could write this book.

When students and friends see how I am using improvisational bead embroidery to heal old wounds, there is an immediate strong temptation to look at the work and "play psychologist" with it. They, and sometimes I too, want to figure out what everything means, and to speculate about why I chose certain colors or made certain patterns, etc. However, I caution them, myself and you not to do that. The healing is not in the interpretation of the work. The healing is in doing the work. The healing happens without conscious awareness. Probably in much the same way that practicing meditation or tai chi calms the body and aligns the spirit, improvisational bead embroidery calms the mind and allows the heart to heal.

I think of these pieces as gifts to me from my heart; a physical path for communication from my heart through the work of my hands, which bypasses my brain. The more intense the issue or the pain, and the more I use sensitive materials in my choices of fabric, beads and embellishments, the more I stand to gain from them.

There's another way to up your gain when working on an "issue piece," and that's to write poems about yourself using your work as inspiration. Here's how: find a quiet chunk of time when you will not be disturbed. Clear a small writing space, but keep your beads and bead embroidery close, where you can see them . Take about 5 minutes to make a list of all the words and phrases which pop into your mind as you look at your beads and your work and the area around you. When you're finished, read through your list and circle the word or phrase which seems the most compelling to you. On another paper, write the words "I am _____". Put the circled word in the blank space. This is the first line of a poem about you. Use some or all of the other words on the list and finish your poem. I often do this exercise several times while I am working on a piece. Sometimes I write the poem on the paper backing, so that it's always with my work. Poems are another way of direct communication from the heart. You may receive your heart's message to you clearly and beautifully by writing poems inspired by your beadwork.

A word now about getting stuck. I, and everyone I know, has had the experience of getting stuck, or of suddenly acquiring an intense dislike of our work. For both situations, the remedy is the same: pick up a bead you love, one you absolutely adore, and sew it somewhere, anywhere, on your work. That's all it will take to get you going again and/or to stop your critical side from making its judgements. More than once while making every single piece you see in this book, I despaired that it was ugly and not worth finishing. I've felt that way at least once about every piece I've made. In addition to picking up a bead I love and sewing it on somewhere, the other thing I do to help is to put my face right in my work. I don't stand back from it, hold it out at arms length, and look at it with a critical eye. And I try not to let others judge my work, or even to see it, while it is in progress. I tend not to show things in progress to those of my friends who always have ideas about how to do it better.

Finding a Path Through Life Changes

I believe that getting more creative with beads, doing improvisational bead embroidery, using your work to heal old wounds and find a path through life changes is a circular route. Doing any one thing in the circle leads us right around to the next. Thus, by allowing ourselves to use our work for healing, we move toward greater creativity. In my experience teaching the techniques of bead embroidery, not many of my students come to class seeing it this way. Instead, they've used their tried-and-true formulas to prepare fabric and beads in the perfectly matched colors of their personal comfort zone. When I tell them about getting creative and the healing powers of working improvisationally with beads, many seem to be surprised, yet intrigued. They may feel a little intimidated by the thought of working without a plan, yet they want to try. Since talking about my work seems to help, here are two more stories, this time about using it to find a path through life changes.

Visiting my brother in California, this is me working on my "menopause" piece one morning in his studio. Note the bright plaid silk fabric which I chose for this project.

39

R. Atkins, 1997

R. Atkins, 1997

"Menopause"
5" diameter, sculptural piece , 3 views (top right, in progress)

40

Although my story about the menopause piece pictured to the left is quite personal, I'm going to share it with you in full, because I think it will help you to better understand the healing power of improvisational bead embroidery and of how the healing, in turn, leads to greater creativity. I started menopause in the early '90s, and by mid-decade hot flashes, night sweats and mood swings were a daily part of my life. I had been single for some time, but was beginning to take up ballroom dancing and had begun dating a little. I began to think that I might be open to the idea of a mate. But in my menopausal state, the thought of being sexually active again frightened me nearly to death. I simply didn't know if I had it in me. You guessed it; I decided to make a piece about my sexuality. On three occasions as I worked, I wrote poems using the model on page 38.

All the time I was beading, I thought it would become a little pouch or bag. But my hands resisted my every attempt to direct it into a square or bag-shaped piece. It wanted to be round and irregular. Finally I got to a place where I just couldn't sew another bead on the fabric (see top right picture on pg. 40). The next morning I woke up inspired to "cup" the piece (by gathering around the circumference), stuff it, sew it to fabric-covered cardboard cut slightly smaller than the shape of the piece, fringe it, and turn it into a small table sculpture (which, looking at it now, reminds me of a breast). As I was stuffing it, I added a picture of a tiger and a bunch of bright confetti. On the underside, I made a small pocket to hold my poems.

In the process of working on this piece and writing the poems, my fear lifted and a joy about myself as a woman took its place. I found a path through menopausal life changes, and came out on the other side a refreshed and happier person. Within a few months I met the "man of my dreams," and found myself open and eager to begin our partnership with a new sense of creative spirit.

As my new relationship grew stronger, we began to consider the question of marriage. Neither of us has been married previously; we're in our 50's; and both of us are quite independent. Faced with another big life change, I decided, of course, to make a piece about it. Here it is, in progress. Since I wanted to make something which could hold small meaningful tokens of our commitment to each other, I decided on a bag shape, and began with the piece shown to

R. Atkins, 2000

"Marriage"
3 ½" x 5 ½", front (in progress), and side

the left. After completing that, I began on the other side, shown below. Then, because I wanted some depth to the bag, I made a pattern for side pieces, which will be joined at center bottom. Next I will line the pieces, perhaps add fringe, and sew the bag parts together. Perhaps it will hang as a sculpture from the buttons on the sides... I'm trying not to control or plan it. Although it is not yet finished, the process of working on it has already helped me with my

R. Atkins, 2000

"Marriage"
3 ½" x 5 ½", other front and side

43

mixed emotions about the possibility of marriage. I have come to a point of commitment about it which feels comfortable, safe, and satisfying.

Things You Can Make with Your Improvisational Bead Embroidery

So far in the pages of this book, you've seen many bags or pouches of different shapes and sizes. You've also seen a wall quilt with bead embroidered squares, a book, and a sculpture. Below are pictures of two "spirit dolls," which I embellished with bead embroidery, and on the following pages, two more books, another framed piece, and some beaded buttons. One thing I have not yet tried is bead embroidered clothing. But I had a student who completed her first square of beadwork and turned it into a pocket on a blazer. Later she made bead embroidered cuffs and covered buttons for it too. Your imagination is the limit to other possibilities.

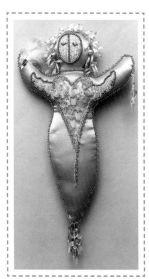

R. Atkins, 1996

"Sweet Dreams"
left, 6" x 8 ½"
spirit doll

"Grieving with Precious Tears"
rt., 6" x 8 ½" spirit doll

I do the improvisational bead embroidery on the body and face first; then cut out the doll, hand-sew her together, and embellish her with fringed hair and edge stitching.

R. Atkins, 1994

R. Atkins, 1996

"I Am a Tree"
left, 2 ½" x 3 ½", mini-book

R. Atkins, 1993

*"Moonlight on My
Rose Garden"*
9" x 12" blank book (detail right)

R. Atkins, 1993

"Stitch Sampler"

left, 4½" x 6", matted & framed

Every time I teach a class, we practice all of the techniques on a 4"
square of fabric. We use a "stew"
of beads, each student contributing
one color. This is my demonstra-
tion sampler, continued
over 5 or 6 classes.

"Beaded Buttons"

below, 1¼" diameter each

I use standard Dritz™ covered
button forms for these buttons,
following the instructions on the
back of the package, and doing my
improvisational bead embroidery
(the same size as the button top)
in the center.

R. Atkins, 1996

R. Atkins, 1996 - 99

Medicine Bags

In the spirit of many native cultures, medicine bags, intended to "protect" or "heal," are especially wonderful when made improvisationally. Making them for myself or as gifts, I embellish and fill them with talismanic things which have special significance to me.

R. Atkins, 1995

"Travel Medicine Bag"
4 ¹/₄" x 4"
front and back views

"Medicine Bags"
about 4" x 4" each
leather

I made these bags for my best friend, myself, and my partner (clockwise from top right) for protection from illnesses. Compare these bags to the one above and note that the bead embroidery is sparse on these bags. It is easier to embroider solid designs on fabric than on leather.

R. Atkins, 1999

Stitch Gallery

Fortunately, there are only a few bead embroidery techniques, and once learned, you can accomplish any "look" you want. Everything you've ever seen, where beads are sewn onto cloth or leather, is done with one or more of these four basic stitches: seed stitch, lazy stitch, couching, and back stitch (or variations thereof).

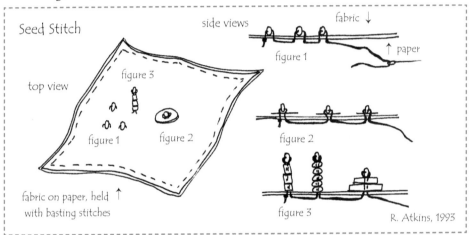

Seed Stitch

Sew to the surface, pick up a single bead, and sew back to the underside (figure 1). When small beads (size 15 - 10 seed beads) are used, the results of this stitch look like "French knots" in thread embroidery. Variations include using the seed stitch to sew on sequins, disc beads, or buttons (figure 2), and to "anchor" stacks (figure 3).

48

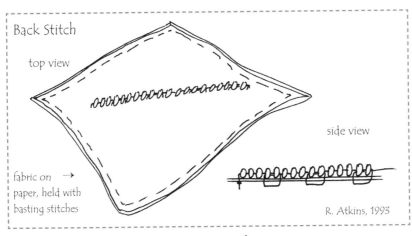

Back Stitch

top view

side view

fabric on →
paper, held with
basting stitches

R. Atkins, 1993

Back Stitch

Sew to surface and string 5 beads on the needle. Lay the beads flat along the fabric in the desired direction, and sew through to the underside at the end of the line of beads. Sew back to the surface again, coming up between the 3rd and 4th beads. Pass the needle through the 4th and 5th beads for the 2nd time. Without sewing to the underside, string 5 more beads on the needle and repeat, "locking" the beads in place by back stitching through the 4th and 5th beads of every 5. Good for long curved or straight lines, I use this stitch more frequently than any other, especially for outlining.

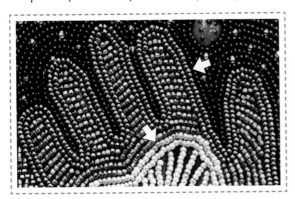

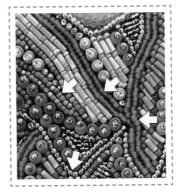

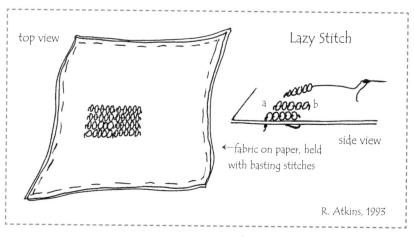

top view

Lazy Stitch

a   b

side view

←fabric on paper, held
with basting stitches

R. Atkins, 1993

Lazy Stitch

Working in columns, sew on 3 to 5 beads at a time. Always bring
the thread to the surface on the "a" side of the column and return to
the back on the "b" side of the column, with the thread running the
width of the column diagonally on the wrong side. I use this stitch
for filling in small areas. For example: after outlining the hand
(page 49, left) in back stitch, I filled the fingers with lazy stitch.
Working in small patches, with the rows of each patch at right angles
to the previous patch, I create a "basket weave" look (below, right).
With a seed bead/bugle bead/seed bead combination, I use the lazy
stitch to make what I call "bugle bead pathways" (below, left).

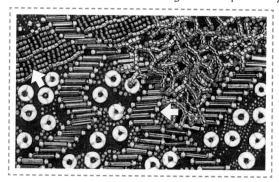

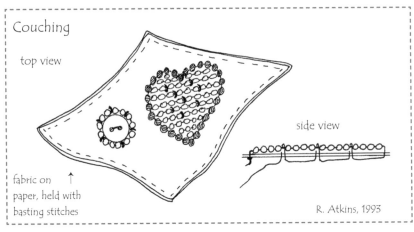

Couching

top view

side view

fabric on ↑
paper, held with
basting stitches

R. Atkins, 1993

Couching

With the thread on the right side, string a line of beads. Sew to the underside at the end of the line. Working back toward the starting point, couch the line of beads to the fabric by sewing to the surface every 3-5 beads, crossing the thread between two beads, and sewing back to the underside. Although in appearance this stitch is inter-changeable with back stitch, I don't use it as much. I like it for making a circle or partial circle of beads around a disc bead or button. I also use it, along with lazy stitch, for filling an outlined area. If the rows are 5 beads long or less, I use lazy stitch. For rows over 5 beads long, I couch the row between every 3 or 4 beads to hold it securely in place.

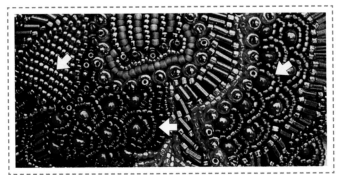

Embellish Your Work with Fringes

Fringing adds movement and texture to your bead embroidery, plus an opportunity to showcase specialty beads. You can decorate a finished piece, such as a purse or doll, with one or more types of fringe. It's also fun to work some of the following fringe techniques directly on your bead embroidery as a textural surface embellishment. Sometimes, I allow the fringe to stick up; other times I couch it down to the piece, as shown below.

"Wildflower Garden"
6" x 6 ½" framed piece, detail

When you look closely at this piece, you can see twisted fringe and kinky fringe, both couched down (white arrows). You can also see various loop fringes and short fringes (pink arrows). These fringe techniques used on flat bead embroidery give it a pleasing raised texture.

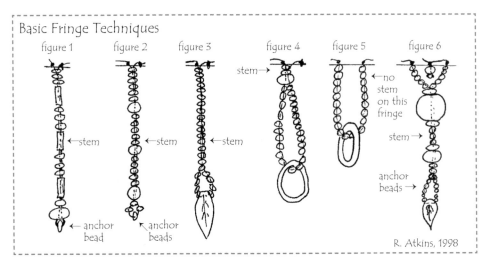

R. Atkins, 1998

Basic Fringe Techniques

To make a simple fringe (figure 1), pass your needle through the whole length of the fringe, select and thread the anchor (or bottom) bead, and stitch back up the stem of the fringe through every bead. To tighten the fringe, grasp the anchor bead in one hand and the stringing thread in the other. Pull on the stringing thread while providing tension on the anchor bead. Knot after every fringe.

For a nice variation (figure 2), string three anchor beads at the end of your fringe to form a little diamond shape. If you want to showcase a dangle or drop bead (figure 3), thread 4 to 6 small beads (size 14 or 15 seed beads work well for this) at the end of the fringe, then the dangle/drop, then an equal number of small beads; then stitch the thread back through the stem of the fringe to the top.

I often use loop fringe to hold rings or charms. The loop may have a short stem (figure 4), or be more like a swing without a stem (figure 5), or be a combination (figure 6). Short loops give a nice textural effect to flat bead embroidery (see "Menopause" on page 40).

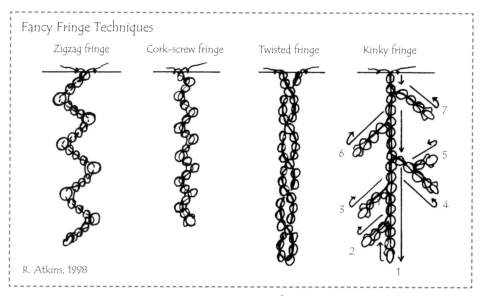

Fancy Fringe Techniques

Zigzag fringe   Cork-screw fringe   Twisted fringe   Kinky fringe

Fancy Fringe Techniques

To make a zigzag fringe, thread beads in an alternating pattern of 3 or 4 small and 1 larger seed bead. After adding the anchor bead, thread back up the stem skipping all of the larger beads. The cork-screw fringe is similar. Using one size of beads, thread to the anchor bead, then back up the stem skipping every other bead. When this fringe is pulled tight, it resembles a little pig's tail or cork-screw.

The secret to the twisted fringe is using a single thread which is large enough to fill the holes of the beads in the fringe. String enough beads so that when doubled back on itself, the loop is slightly longer than you want your fringe to be. Holding the thread close to the end of the string of beads, twist the thread repeatedly in the same direction. Test for sufficient twisting by bringing the twisted end to the top of the fringe. While stitching through the fabric to the back side and knotting, don't let go of the twisted end of the thread or you'll loose the twist.

Kinky fringe (sometimes called "branch fringe") makes a rich and thick fringe. When couched down on the surface of your bead embroidery, it creates texture (see "Wildflower Garden," pg. 52) or doll hair (see "Sweet Dreams," pg. 44). Begin by stringing the entire stem of the fringe, ending with anchor bead #1. Thread back up a few beads in the stem. Add a few beads and anchor bead #2; then thread back through the branch you just made and back up the stem a little way. Work your way up the stem, creating branches, and sub-branches (see #5). Tighten the tension after each branch.

"Marriage Bag"

detail showing
fringe

This photo shows how I tend to mix different types of fringing techniques with many different charms and beads to create a full, rich looking fringe.

R. Atkins, 2000

55

Closing Thoughts

If these pages, which have flowed out of my teaching and my experience, inspire you to try improvisational bead embroidery, I will be satisfied. Whether you do it just for fun, as an experiment in getting more creative with beads, or with the added incentive of healing an old wound or finding a path through a life change - whatever your motivation - I believe you will be glad for the time you gave it and pleased with your results.

A Few Special Resources

"Dibs, In Search of Self," by Virginia M. Axline, c. 1964 - a case history of the healing of a young boy through play therapy; a book I read every year or so for inspiration and a lesson in how to play.

"The Artist's Way, A Spiritual Path to Higher Creativity," by Julia Cameron, c. 1992 - an "inner workbook" that explores spirit, self, and creativity through writing, visualization, ritual, and imagination.

"Living Color, A Writer Paints Her World," by Natalie Goldberg, c. 1997 - about the need to "step out of form," to express inner self and to find harmony through art; a book to inspire again and again.

"West Wind," by Mary Oliver, c. 1997 - this book of poems (and all her others as well) gives me a sense of spiritual well being and confidence, which in turn allows my creativity to open more fully.

About My Background

I grew up in Minnesota, where I earned a Masters Degree in Counseling Psychology at the U of MN. I worked as a youth counselor for 7 years, moved to the West Coast and changed careers to theatre management for 15 years, then got hooked on beads. That was in 1987; ever since then, they've been my passion! I continue to research and teach about beads, and to develop my own artistic style with them.